Leadership

A Practical Guide on Self-Development and How to be a Great Leader and Influence People

C.J. Stranberg

ISBN-13: 978-1507706350

ISBN-10: 1507706359

www.mritchi.com

CONTENTS

INTRODUCTION

Like many people, you probably look up to someone who exemplifies good leadership.

You may have seen the person speak in public settings and witnessed his power and impact on those whom he leads. You may have stood in amazement and admiration at how this individual effectively led an organization, providing motivation around people and spreading positive energy with everyone – even during the hardest of times.

In your mind, you may have said "Wow! What a natural leader. I can never imagine myself doing something like that."

And so this is a serious question that begs to be answered: Are leaders really born or made?

This book aims to demonstrate that anyone – including you – can be a leader.

Leadership: A Practical Guide on Self-Development and How to be a Great Leader and Influence People provides you with what you need to know so you can have better, clearer understanding regarding the nature and essence of leadership. You will also learn the traits and skills that will help nurture the leader in you.

Because, yes, anyone can be a leader! Acquiring the needed knowledge and skills will boost your ability and confidence to lead others.

So whether you have been thrust into the position by default (you may have started a business) or by appointment (you may have been promoted in your work or voted by others in your organization), there is no escaping leadership.

By reading this book and applying the principles taught herein, you can be the best leader that you have always wanted to be.

« CHAPTER 1 »

A Closer Look at Leadership

A quick check on the dictionary will reveal that the word "lead" means many things. Some of the basic definitions include "to guide or direct in a course" and "to show the way to (an individual or organization) by going with or ahead."

Thus, a leader performs a very crucial role in any business or organization. Leadership is the art of leading people into achieving a common goal and it takes skills, intelligence, and experience to do it right. Not every person who gets called to fill such a position has the needed qualities and traits to succeed in the task. Frankly, it can even be said that leaders even vary in their understanding and methods about how to get the job done.

The following illustration may be helpful in identifying what leadership is and what it is not:

Shepherd vs. Sheep Herder

There is significant difference between a shepherd and a sheep herder. While both have similar duties (to tend to their sheep), they have contrasting ways in approaching their assignments.

For instance, a shepherd leads his sheep from the front. He knows his sheep well (even by name), has earned their confidence, and has developed a good relationship with them. The sheep know him too and can readily recognize his voice. They follow him when he gives instructions. He, in turn, is willing to defend and protect the flock whenever the situation calls for it.

The sheep herder, on the other hand, is exactly the opposite of all that. He doesn't care about the sheep and drives them from the back. He often has to talk loudly to them because they do not listen or obey his commands. He uses fear and threats to make them do what he wants. He will run away and leave the flock in case the wolves start coming.

No wonder, a sheep herder sometimes go by the derogatory name "hireling," meaning someone "who only works for pay."

What Kind of Leader Are You?

First off, how would you describe yourself as a person? What values are important for you? What are your strengths and weaknesses?

Your perception of who you are will play a vital role in defining who you can become as a leader. If you want to be effective in what you do (shepherd) and are not merely aiming to get the job over with so you can collect your reward (sheep herder), you should be willing to make certain changes in the way act and the way think. You need to have the right set of values as a person so you can pass the same positive attitude among those who follow you.

To lead is indeed not an easy feat but when done the right way, it can be a rewarding experience – not only for you but for those you will influence along the way.

With effective leadership, you will be able to, as Dolly Parton eloquently described, inspire others to "dream more, learn more, do more and become more."

« CHAPTER 2 »

What Makes a Good Leader

Zig Ziglar, a popular motivational speaker and best-selling author, plainly taught "Your attitude, not your aptitude, will determine your altitude."

In this chapter, you will learn about the attributes common among successful leaders. You may feel a little overwhelmed while reading this since you will get to pinpoint some of your personal flaws but do not be too troubled about it.

Recognize that there are no such things as perfect leaders and besides, many of these traits can be learned. As with driving, skiing, drawing, cooking, and many other skills and talents, it all starts with desire. With constant effort and practice, leadership qualities can definitely be cultivated.

1. A good leader is organized.

A commendable leader knows the value of being organized. He knows his priorities, goals, and vision (more on that on the next chapter). He stays focused on the important matters without losing sight on seemingly-little things. Even his office is well-arranged. Humorous as it may sound, there is great truth in the wall sign that says "A cluttered desk is a sign of a cluttered mind."

2. A good leader sees the good in people.

Jonas Falk, CEO of OrganicLife, said that "Leadership is the ability to take an average team of individuals and transform them into superstars. The best leader is the one who inspires his workers to achieve greatness each and every day."

The good leader believes in the potential of those he works with and helps them realize it. He is, in a way, a coach and a cheer leader.

3. A good leader leads, not manipulates.

As with the shepherd and sheep herder analogy on the previous chapter, a real leader does not rely on fear. Although he knows he has to act authoritatively at times, he does not feel compelled to use his position to manipulate others to complete the tasks at hand. He simply shows the way and leads his people towards the right direction.

4. A good leader motivates.

Proper motivation is always necessary and the good leader often provides that. Those working with an ideal leader know that they are being led by someone who is there to help and support them – not harass them. They know that their leader is patient and will always encourage them. He is not a "baby sitter" who has to dictate everything that needs to be done, he simply gives clear explanations and assures his people that they can do it.

5. A good leader promotes open communication.

Communication is crucial for a business or organization to do productive work together and to function with greater efficiency. Although a leader often needs to talk with his members, he should also know when to stop. He should be willing to listen and learn from others. He weighs on people's opinions and suggestions before arriving at a conclusion. During concerns and conflicts, he is not quick to judge but takes the time to hear out both sides.

6. A good leader sets an example.

Finally, an excellent leader always sets a good example. He should practice what he preaches. He also makes it a point to fulfill commitments and keep promises. This will help him establish a reputation of consistency and integrity – both of which are imperative if he desires to earn people's trust.

« CHAPTER 3 »

Leading by Example

Everyone hates that boss who demands employees to arrive early but always comes in late. Or the supervisor who always preaches against spending too much time on the Internet but posts photos on his personal social media account during working hours.

In short, you, as a leader, are in a position where those around you are expecting you to set a good example. If you want to be effective in fulfilling your responsibilities, you can never afford to have a "do what I say, but not what I do" attitude.

You have to walk your talk. It is the only way to gain the confidence and trust of your people. In many ways, the life you live is the lesson you teach. Action is indeed more powerful than words and what people see you do will have a greater impact than what you say.

"All leadership," according to **John C. Maxwell** "is influence" and you need to be a role model in order to have a positive influence among those you lead.

Albert Einstein also gave emphasis to the importance of this principle when he said "Example isn't another way to teach — it is the only way to teach." Similarly, **Sun Tzu** taught "A leader leads by example not by force." You can count on people doing the right things even when you're not around, not because they fear you but because they respect you enough and sincerely want to live up to your expectations.

Bad Effects of a Leader's Bad Example

As you can probably picture by now, negative implications always follows negative leadership example.

Unifying a team can be a constant struggle. People are always less than willing to cooperate. Motivating a group to work together towards a common goal can be a pertinent problem. Bluntly said, people do not enjoy being led by a hypocrite.

According to a recent study, those who stay in a work environment with such a leader are only 1) afraid to go through the entire job hunt process all over again and 2) only work for the salary. In some instances, expected results are still met but it's always certain that winning everyone's heart will be out of the picture.

The group or business will not have a clear direction if they are not united in purpose.

You Do Not Want To Be THAT Leader

No leader wants to be in that type of scenario. This can be avoided if you will often look inwards, honestly evaluating your behavior and performance as a leader. Examine yourself and ask if there have been instances in the past when you have not fulfilled a promise or have broken the very rules you have set. Do your best to amend and prevent such mistakes. Apologize in case you fall short of everyone's expectations. One of the marks of a true leader is that he or she is not afraid to admit his errors and make an apology when necessary.

Your followers will only believe you if they are seeing your sincere effort to be true to your words. Motivating people will be easier. Your visions will promote enthusiasm. Strengthening everyone within the team will come naturally. Disappointments, cynicism, and doubt can be prevented.

All of this will come as an outcome of showing a firm commitment in what you say. Your strength of character will serve as an inspiration. Showing dependability increases your moral authority. Be proactive when you encounter challenges and in return, you can expect the same from others.

In a wider scope, author and speaker **Scott Berkun** has said "Leadership comes from integrity... Just by providing a good example as a parent, a friend, a neighbor makes it possible for other people to see better ways to do things. Leadership does not need to be a dramatic, fist in the air and trumpets blaring activity.

« CHAPTER 4 »

The Importance of Vision in Leading

One scriptural passage from the Old Testament says "Where there is no vision, the people perish (Proverbs 29:18)." The same can actually be said about companies big and small. Without vision and direction, any business will eventually fail.

This is where the work of a leader comes in. His job is to align the company in the same path by painting a clear picture of what they want to achieve together. In short, a leader is in charge of helping creating a common vision, defining the details, and uniting everyone involved towards hitting the goal.

Rosabeth Moss Kanter gave a good definition of the word when she said "A vision is not just a picture of what could be; it is an appeal to our better selves, a call to become something more."

Vision First, Strategy Second

Needless to say, having a vision brings numerous benefits to any business or organization. With it in place, strategic planning can be done with greater accuracy. Strategy, while extremely important, only comes second in terms of priority. Experienced leaders will always tell you that even the best strategies will amount to nothing without a solid vision.

Building a Shared Vision

If you noticed in the second paragraph of this chapter, the word "helping" is added on the topic of vision creation. While some leaders make it their sole responsibility to create a vision for the entire organization and then present it afterwards to their members, there are those who do this task differently.

What they do is to go the extra mile, involving everyone in the team by gathering their insights and then merging them to form one concrete plan. Leadership coaching experts point out that this type of approach is more effective because people feel greater responsibility and ownership of the vision.

A story is told of a customer who was pleasantly surprised with how staff members took excellent care of him when he checked in to a hotel. They went beyond providing the usual service of carrying his things and taking him to his room. They showed genuine concern, greeted him by name, always asked if he needed any help, showed him the convention room (where the guest will be holding a conference the next day) – all without being asked and all without supervision of the management.

This didn't escape the client's attention and he took the time to speak with the hotel manager when he got the chance. He asked about their "secret formula" of making all these wonderful things happen in their hotel. The manager, smiling, replied that he involved everyone in creating the mission and vision. Thus, the employees were more eager to execute all the things within their plan because it was them that helped form it in the first place. They are not merely being told what to do – they decided what needed to be done.

This is perhaps a great demonstration of what **Antoine de Saint-Exupery** meant when he said "If you want to build a ship, don't herd people together to collect wood and don't assign them tasks and work, but rather teach them to long for the endless immensity of the sea."

« CHAPTER 5 »

A Great Leader Is a Great Communicator

It was author **Ken Blanchard** who popularized the catchy but truthful quote that says "Feedback is the breakfast of champions."

As mentioned in one of the previous chapters, a good leader promotes open communication. Even if you're exceptional in what you do, you can't afford to do a one-man-show. Remember that your chief function is simply to guide, not to do everything the way you want it done, dismissing other's insights or feelings.

Paying attention to suggestions and comments can be for your own benefit, whether you are leading a business, a political party, an athletic team, or even a family. Accordingly, you have to know how to put your thoughts across without the risk of being misunderstood.

Here are some ideas to enrich your communication skills:

1. Carefully choose your words (and tone).

Never assume that you have the right to be tactless just because you are the leader. Being careful with the words you say is most effective. Plan and practice what you're going to say. Your delivery is just as important as the words you speak so make sure that both are able to convey the same message. Remember that there are many ways to express things.

2. Praise people.

The "Dealing with Difficulties" chapter tells us that praising achievements is something you should do frequently. This should be done both in public and private. People love to know that their efforts are being acknowledged by their leaders. Be sincere when you commend individuals. People can usually tell the difference between a genuine praise and a fake one.

Retain the same positive tone when giving suggestions. Show that you are truly concerned about pushing them towards their full potential. In short, be constructive. Feel free to offer help whenever appropriate. Uplifting words can be a potent motivational tool.

3. Do not beat around the bush.

Be specific when laying out details or when giving instructions. "Be more responsible" can mean a lot of things so don't sugarcoat your message and say it as it is. More often than not, "We want reports to be delivered on time" will bring better outcome. When setting a goal, specify target figures and relate as much information as necessary.

4. Encourage two-way communication.

The thing about many leaders is that they sometimes assume communication has taken place when the contrary has just happened. The leader stood up, spoke for about an hour or so, and then dismissed the meeting as he sat down.

The sides of both the leader and the team should be heard during gatherings. Know when and how to listen. Open the floor for questions. Ask people for suggestions. Your members may see certain aspects of the topic at hand in a different light than you do. You might have missed a few things here and there and so being open to other's viewpoints can be a valuable asset.

5. Restate.

When done properly, restating the comments or questions is a skill that confirms you clearly understood the speaker. Rephrase what you heard in your own words to make sure that you got it right. Be cautious and respectful when doing this though so that it doesn't sound demeaning to the individual.

6. Keep things confidential.

A responsible leader never divulges things that he or she knows should be confidential. Earn the trust of your team by not sharing off-the-record details – especially if you've promised that you will keep the matter secret.

Communication truly precedes success.

Mastering this art is a must for anyone who wants to be an efficient leader. It takes a lot of practice and preparation but the payoff at the end will always be worth it.

« CHAPTER 6 »

Managing Inner and Outer Conflict

Syrian philosopher **Publilius Syrus** is often quoted for saying "Anyone can hold the helm when the sea is calm."

The same can be said regarding leadership.

While anyone can be elected or appointed as a leader, only those who have strong will and zealous enough will stay standing once the tides begin to rise.

Sooner or later, you will encounter problems while you are serving as a leader. Your behavior during these hard times will not only reflect your inner character but will, most importantly, affect everyone within your sphere of influence. Ultimately, the behavior of your workers and direction of your organization will depend on how you act or react as you face challenges.

So how do you respond when you have to deal with difficult situations? Here are some ideas taken straight from leadership development training courses.

Diagnose Before You Prescribe

Just as a good doctor will not give any prescriptions until after diagnosing the patient, you, the leader, should likewise take the time to examine problems at hand before coming up with effective solutions.

Do not make the mistake of immediately jumping into conclusions. Setbacks usually take a turn for the worse when leaders overreact to them. It's always better to ask questions first and gather as much information as you can so you can make proper analysis of the situation. Thus, arriving at an ideal resolution will be possible.

See Things Half-Full

Although no one desires difficulties, your behavior as you meet them is the most crucial. It's either you regard them as stepping stones or stumbling blocks on your road to success.

Benjamin Franklin summed it up best when he spoke "While we may not be able to control all that happens to us, we can control what happens inside of us."

Positive energy, much like its negative counterpart, is pretty contagious. Your workers will take notice if you are able to stay optimistic during crisis and they will be affected by it. So instead of being discouraged, keep your cool, stay cheerful and show confidence in your team. Doing so will bring greater productivity and enthusiasm even in the middle of difficulties.

"Believe it is possible to solve your problem" states **Norman Vincent Peale**. "Tremendous things happen to the believer. So believe the answer will come. It will."

Praise in Public, Correct in Private

Correcting people is often inevitable. When things go wrong or when an individual does deviate from the right direction (despite repeated guidance and warning), then correction must be done.

One thing you need to understand about this though is that no one wants to get reprimanded in front of his or her peers – especially if the rebuke is sharp. For this reason, leadership coaching professionals recommend that the leader should sit down with the individual for a private conversation. People respond more positively to correction when they are not humiliated in front of others.

So the rule is pretty simple – praise people in public (more about this on the next chapter), but talk to them in private if corrective measures are necessary.

« CHAPTER 7 »

Making the Right Decisions

It may not sound like an exciting idea but you, the leader, will often have to make difficult decisions during your term as a leader.

There are certain instances when your organization, team, or business will depend on your judgment in deciding on a specific direction or course of action. This is never a simple responsibility, especially because you will need to balance emotion and reason. Adapting to change and facing uncertainty can be daunting for most – and it is your job to make the right move.

Besides, the willingness "to make decisions," according to **General George S. Patton,** is "the most important quality in a good leader.

Timing Is Everything

The importance of proper timing in decision-making could never be overemphasized. In many ways, they are often considered as the most crucial factor. You have to know that even the most well-meaning decisions can go wrong if the timing is not right.

You have to analyze the matter at hand and then decide whether you should immediately take action or not. There are circumstances when it is a wiser idea to collect and study information first. Distinguishing the difference between proceeding and not going ahead at the precise moment is undeniably vital. You have to assess the situation, too, being careful not to take a lot of time in making your decision. Sometimes a delayed decision will not have as much impact as desired.

Announce the Decision

Once you have made your mind, make sure that you communicate the decision to the concerned parties. This is important to show respect to your team so that they are aware about your final decision. Some of them may have been involved in the decision making process that's why it makes perfect sense to let them know. Many of them may have offered different suggestions and ideas. Inform them about which decision finally felt right for you.

Also, enumerate all the benefits you can see regarding this direction you're planning to take.

This is intended to help boost everyone's enthusiasm about it.

Stay Proactive Regardless of the Outcome

There will be times when you will wonder whether you have made the right call or not. Sometimes negative results come regardless of your best efforts. Do not waste time blaming yourself (or anyone else) when that happens. It is much better to stay proactive than reactive.

Take control of the situation by evaluating what needs to be done and then go for the best option. Present the problem to those you lead and, when appropriate, ask them for help as you come up with a plan to deal with the consequences.

Again, do not be so hard on yourself in case mistakes occur. Take comfort from this relevant quote by an unknown author which says "Good decisions come from experience, and experience comes from bad decisions."

Be ready to take risks and do not be discouraged in case you encounter failure. Most often than not, it is never too late to rescue a situation. Just take it as a learning experience and do your best to avoid the same errors in the future.

« CHAPTER 8 »

Adapting with Change

An old Chinese proverb teaches "The wise adapts themselves to circumstances, as water molds itself to the pitcher."

Brilliant leaders have that characteristic. They recognize change and adapt well to it as necessary. Although majority of people dread change, it is often unavoidable and those who take control of the circumstances and go with the flow are those who reap the benefits. As the old saying goes, "The only thing that's permanent is change" that's why those who tend to accept it are more likely to make needed steps.

Defined by the dictionary as "the ability to adjust oneself readily to different conditions," adaptability is definitely one of the key components of quality leadership.

You have to be ready, calm, and skillful in coping with crisis and emergencies. When problems arise, you should know how to analyze the situation and be able to come up with the best solutions. In the end, meeting the needs and achieving the purpose of your organization is what matters most.

Refer to the Rules – But Don't be Confined In Them

In certain circumstances, referring to the organizations rules can be the way to resolve difficulties. Check out the existing guidelines and see if there is anything that provides light to the situations you are currently having.

However, be sure that you also keep an open mind. Think outside the box and you might surprise even yourself. Revolutionary Apple Corporation founder **Steve Jobs** used to preach that "innovation distinguishes between a leader and a follower."

The Value of Listening

Do not be too quick to dismiss ideas and opinions of those around you. Some leaders have the mindset that it is often easier to think of solutions themselves and not involve others at all. This, of course, is a wrong way to look at things.

Be attentive to others' suggestions and you will probably learn a great deal. Listen, analyze, and listen again. Negativity kills good ideas and so be sure not to take that direction – perhaps especially when you think you've got everything all figured out.

Break Your Routine

This may sound too simple for a suggestion but you have to realize that sometimes, the simple things bring the best outcome. Try doing things differently just to get a fresher perspective in what you do.

Embrace Change

Instead of being the first one to show signs of hesitance in the group, be the example by proving that you are excited and open-minded. If a new system or technology is introduced in your field, be the first one to try it. Learn it and share your enthusiasm with others. You will see that this is a more effective way of motivating your people rather than pushing them to do it when you yourself are cynical about the entire idea.

Encouraging Others

The same positivity should show whenever you have to implement change for good. Address your team's uncertainty by helping them see the advantages that can be seen and experienced.

When delegating duties, you can probably consider assigning work based on the interest and skills of your group members just to make the transition a little less painful for everyone. When recruiting or hiring new people, go for individuals with skills or experience you may not have yet in the group.

Do not think twice about restructuring your organization or group if it will ultimately lead to the best benefits.

Flexibility Always Wins

The entire point of the matter can be summed up in Marc Andreessen's immortal three words - "adaptability is key." Albert Einstein, famed physicist, said "The measure of intelligence is the ability to change."

American historian Drew Gilpin Faust similarly taught "The ability to recognize opportunities and move in new – and sometimes unexpected – directions will benefit you no matter your interests or aspirations."

Keep these wise words in mind and you will discover that you will be less of a whiner next time you come across change.

« CHAPTER 9 »

The Power of Effective Delegation

Delegation is probably one of the toughest tasks of a leader. In fact, there are some leaders who do not bother doing it at all. They do not share the workload with others and simply do the tasks themselves. Part of the reason for the hesitance is that some leaders think that they can do certain jobs better than others and so delegating may not sound like a sensible idea in the outset. Still, it is a sad fact that those who insist on running a one-man company (or organization) are bound to feel more stressed and eventually get unsatisfactory results.

This, of course, is the big difference between leadership and self-deception.

The Wisdom of Delegation

As **Gen. Omar Bradley** pointed out "The greatness of a leader is measured by the achievements of the led. This is the ultimate test of his effectiveness."

By delegation, you are not only making your life easier – you are also developing future leaders in the process. So while delegation may not always be easy, it is something that good leaders will always do.

Delegating responsibilities with others come with several advantages. To begin with, you will have lesser work to do if you entrust certain tasks with your workers. As mentioned, you will be able to develop others as you ask them to act on your behalf. Finally, things can still get going even in your absence.

Here are the steps you need to make to get delegation done the right way:

1. Explain the assignment clearly.

Spell out your expectations, break down the assignments and make sure everyone understands the goal. It is also important to ensure that all departments working on the project are well-coordinated.

Let others take care of the project's details. Allowing a little freedom may be a bit tricky but doing that encourages initiative and creativity.

Setting a clear deadline is also important.

2. Hold them accountable.

After passing the bucket, your next move is to clarify that you will hold the assigned person (or persons) fully accountable. Confirm his or her commitment by saying something like "Do I have you word that you will do your best for this task?"

A responsible individual will be up for the challenge, knowing that he has given his commitment to something worth-doing.

3. Make appropriate follow-ups.

Ideally, you should do a follow-up with the person before the day of the deadline. This gives you an opportunity to check the progress, do a bit of evaluation, make suggestions and direct any needed changes so that the target can still be hit in case certain challenges are encountered. Provide encouragement and further coaching whenever necessary.

4. Check again on the deadline.

Commend the person if the task is successfully completed. Offer rewards or recognition if needed. If the goal is not achieved, try to make the best of the situation by having an honest evaluation – what went wrong and why, what can be learned from the experience, what can be done next time to avoid the same errors.

By doing these things, you will be able to demonstrate the value of hard work and commitment.

« CHAPTER 10 »

Mentoring Others

It has been said that one of the surest indicators of a good leader is not only in the way he or she leads an organization but whether or not he or she has trained a competent replacement.

In **Bob Goshen**'s words, "Leaders... should influence others... in such a way that it builds people up, encourages and edifies them so they can duplicate this attitude in others."

Thus, mentoring is also a skill you should strive to master. Effective mentoring helps bring out the best in people and makes it possible for them to correctly perform assigned duties.

Mentoring Defined

The dictionary defines "mentor" as a "wise and trusted counselor or teacher" or an "influential senior sponsor or supporter."

Eric Parsloe dug deeper on this topic and explained that mentoring is "to support and encourage people to manage their own learning in order that they may maximize their potential, develop their skills, improve their performance and become the person they want to be."

Qualities of a Good Mentor

As you take on the responsibility of mentoring others, you should know how to do it the right way. You should also possess basic attributes in order to fulfill your duties properly.

First and foremost, you should be willing to impart your knowledge and experiences. Also, you should be someone who actually enjoys motivating people. Are you also good in listening and in handling difficult questions? If so, then you have some of the qualities of a capable mentor.

Assessing the Mentee's Strengths and Weaknesses

Evaluating the mentee's strong and weak points will help you fulfill your responsibilities better. Knowing more about his or her personality, including his or her likes and interests, will allow you to determine which approach will be most effective. This will be an advantage for both parties because you will be able to do your job well and the learner will progress quicker, too.

Simplify and Personalize

Once you're done assessing the capabilities and character of your mentee, then you will know how to get your message across.

If you can, try not to go heavy on jargons and acronyms because that can be a bit confusing for a beginner. Use simple words and then think of ways you can relate the subject matter to his or her points of interests. Your lesson will have a more lasting effect if you take that route.

Involving Learners

When teaching individuals, always remember these wise words from **Benjamin Franklin**: "Tell me and I forget, teach me and I may remember, involve me and I learn."

Although telling and showing are important parts of the teaching process, involving learners is absolutely crucial. To illustrate the point, explaining the functions or even demonstrating how to use a new software will never bring you the same results as allowing your 'student' to play around with it.

When people are involved, they learn and improve faster compared with simply listening to a lecturer.

Other Pointers for the Mentor

Preparation is a key factor for successful mentoring.

During your mentoring session, spend some time to practice with the mentee. This will give you the opportunity to see if the learner has truly understood what you just taught.

Give assignments at the end of the meeting and – to show them that you mean business - remind them that you will follow up with it on the next session.

Conclusion

In his book **The Witch of Portobello**, famous author **Paulo Coelho** wrote that "a teacher... isn't someone who teaches something, but someone who inspires the student to give of her best in order to discover what she already knows."

Being a mentor is truly a noble work and it is your privilege as a leader to step into those shoes as opportunities arise from time to time.

« CHAPTER 11 »

Strategies for Positive Employee Recognition

Appreciating the efforts of those around you can be a wonderful way to help them stay enthusiastic in what they do. According to **Gerard C. Eakedale**, "Recognition is the greatest motivator."

Your employees or members will find it more enjoyable to work with you if you, their leader, take the time to acknowledge their achievements. Doing so helps you retain people better and keep them excited at any tasks at hand. As a result, you will be able to achieve more of your goals as a company or organization.

Here are some simple ways to show gratitude for your workers:

1. Give rewards.

This is the most common form of employee recognition. You can, for instance, offer cash rewards to those who really work hard and hit the target. Incentives are usually hard to resist and you can expect that people will exert their best efforts for your goals. A caution here, however, is that you set the rules clearly so that no one will feel

2. Pick an "Employee of the Month."

Of course, praising outstanding individuals do not always have to cost you some money. A simpler way to do this is to honor achievers with "Employee of the Month" awards. Make it a tradition to announce the name of the chosen person yourself. Give reasons why he or she was chosen. Post a picture of the person in a prominent spot in your office. The beauty of doing this on a monthly basis is that everyone eventually gets the chance to be the featured employee.

3. Remember special occasions.

As a leader, you can't afford to forget birthdays. Simple, personalized gifts are usually memorable. For example, a balloon and a cake may be cheap but buying those for a birthday celebrant can be a fantastic idea. Does your employee love basketball? Add a t-shirt of his favorite team in your gift. Is she into music? Why not give a CD or concert ticket of her favorite band?

In short, you have to know your people well to do this the right way. Also, make sure to mark your calendar (or assign someone to remind you) so that you are aware about upcoming occasions at least a week in advance. That way, you have ample time to prepare for it.

Aside from birthdays, work anniversaries and weddings are some special dates you should also pay attention to.

4. Say "thank you" and mean it.

Sometimes, saying a simple "Thank you for a job well-done" or "You really did good today. Keep it up!" can brighten up the day of a tired employee. Look for reasons to thank people and be sincere when you express your gratitude. They will appreciate such encouraging words from their leader.

« CHAPTER 12 »

Once a Leader, Always a Learner

"Leadership and learning," according to former American president **John F. Kennedy**, "are indispensable to each other."

Indeed, learning is one of the prerequisites of becoming a remarkable leader.

Excellent leaders are lifelong learners. With learning comes improvement and with your personal growth, you and your organization reap the benefits. You will increase your capability to guide, teach, motivate, communicate, and even to build relationships.

Anthony D'Angelo captured the essence of this point when he counseled "Develop a passion for learning. If you do, you will never cease to grow."

With this in mind, it simply follows that those who tend to have a healthy enthusiasm towards learning get to become good leaders themselves. You should always look for opportunities to gain knowledge in every possible way.

Read A Lot

Reading should be one of the top hobbies of a serious leader. Books about leadership can be helpful in giving you insights about your roles and responsibilities. In addition to printed books, you can also check out e-books and relevant websites about the topic.

Moreover, if you are involved in managing a company (whether big or small), you should likewise learn as much as you can about your niche. For example, if you are in the business of printing shirts, then you have to be an expert in that. Find information about the latest technology and techniques. This will not only bring business growth and give you competitive edge but it will help establish your reputation as an authority in your niche.

Attend Workshops and Seminars

Other than books, workshops and seminars can be great sources of information. Listening to industry experts will allow you to discover important facts you might not learn on your own. Motivational speakers will help you get some well-needed boost, especially if you are feeling overwhelmed with your duties.

Other Possible Sources of Learning

Again, your job is to be open to every possible source of knowledge.

In most cases, this includes studying your competition. Business leaders make it a point to analyze other companies to ensure that they can always implement the best practices. Avoiding mistakes will also be easier in the long run if you are a keen observer of trends – not only of your own company but also those of others.

Accordingly, you should always have open ears for those you lead. Do not be too swallowed up in books and workshops that you neglect the significance of listening to those around you. Comments and suggestions from others can be precious. You will grow as an organization if two-way communication is encouraged.

Learning is an Investment

"An investment in knowledge," according to **Benjamin Franklin**, "pays the best interest." On the other hand, it was **Leonardo da Vinci** who spoke "Learning never exhausts the mind."

Conclusion

John C. Maxwell often taught "Leadership is not about titles, positions or flowcharts. It is about one life influencing another."

You, as a leader, will have the unique privilege of rendering your service for the good of an organization. Much like a sports coach, your job is not merely to drive your team to victory but to utilize the skills and strengths of your members and helping them to function effectively as a cohesive unit – regardless of the obstacles that lie ahead.

Remember the words of **Ronald Reagan**: "The greatest leader is not necessarily the one who does the greatest things. He is the one that gets the people to do the greatest things."

As you exhibit positive leadership qualities, serve with pure motives and lead others into implementing the right vision, you will see commendable improvements in your organization.

Encountering setbacks is always a part of the experience but if you don't let them bring you down, it can be a way to strengthen all your members. You may even learn a lesson or two along the way – and those lessons can eventually be used so you can avoid making the same mistakes in the future.

You have good attributes within you and now you need to cultivate them so you can grow and lead others better.

"You are good but it is not enough just to be good," religious leader **Gordon B. Hinckley** pointed out. "You must be good for something. You must contribute to the good of the world. The world must be a better place for your presence. And the good that is in you must be spread to others."

www.ingramcontent.com/pod-product-compliance
Lightning Source LLC
Chambersburg PA
CBHW071005180526
45168CB00003B/1299